To dogs. Is there anything better than dogs? Also to Taylor, Jen, Jake, and Liz,
who put up with me always wanting to talk about dogs.—J.T.

For all those who love their pets unconditionally.—M.L.

Since the publication of this book, beloved German shepherd Champ Biden has passed away.
We dedicate this book to his memory.
Champ Biden (2008–21)

Major Makes History: From the Shelter to the White House
Text copyright © 2021 by Jill Twiss
Illustrations copyright © 2021 by Maribel Lechuga
All rights reserved. Printed in the United States of America.
No part of this book may be used or reproduced in any manner whatsoever without written permission except
in the case of brief quotations embodied in critical articles and reviews. For information address HarperCollins
Children's Books, a division of HarperCollins Publishers, 195 Broadway, New York, NY 10007.
www.harpercollinschildrens.com

ISBN 978-0-06-311876-8

The artist used Adobe Photoshop to create the digital illustrations for this book.
Design by Chelsea C. Donaldson and Honee Jang
21 22 23 24 25 PC 10 9 8 7 6 5 4 3 2 1
❖
First Edition

MAJOR MAKES HISTORY
From the Shelter to the White House

By Jill Twiss

Illustrated by Maribel Lechuga

HARPER

An Imprint of HarperCollins*Publishers*

Hi, friends! My name is Major, and I'm going to tell you how I rescued a president. But wait, I'm getting ahead of myself . . . First, let me tell you about me!

I am a dog, but you could probably tell that already.
You seem pretty on the ball, for a person.

Actually, I am a German shepherd, which some people say means
I'm loyal and courageous. I think it means I'm a really good friend.

Right now, I live in a *very* fancy house called the White House. I live here with the president of the United States, the first lady, and my good pal Champ.

But I didn't always live in such a swanky place. When I was a puppy, my brothers and sisters and I didn't have a family who could take care of us, so we were left at an animal shelter.

An animal shelter is for pets who do not have homes yet. It's also a place where dogs like me can rescue the families that need us.

It was at that shelter where all the fun started!
You know how sometimes you meet someone and you just
know you're gonna be best friends? Well, that was me and Joe.

When Joe walked into the shelter, I noticed him right away. I could tell
that he was missing something, and I had a sneaking suspicion that
"something" might be me. I ran up to take a good sniff and say hello.

"Ruff ruff!" I said.

"I know!" said Joe.

"Bark bark ruff, bark bark RUFF RUFF RUFF," I said.

"Sometimes I feel exactly the same way," said Joe.

"BARK BARK BARK BARK!" I barked.

"Yes," said Joe thoughtfully. "I think I will call you Major."

And then I saw a sparkle in his eyes. That was when I knew
I was going to rescue Joe Biden.

How do you rescue a person, you ask?
Good question.

First, you sniff them out to make sure
they're a good fit.
(And when you know, you know!)

If they pass the sniff test, you go home with them—just to try things out. After all, taking care of a person isn't easy.

You play games with your person, like **Peeing on Every Good Spot in the Yard** or **Guess Who Hid My Very Best Toy in Your Bed?**

You learn that W-A-L-K means—woo-hoo!!—it is
time to take your person outside!

You do your best to sit when your person asks you to (even if you don't feel like it AT ALL). That's because sometimes you do things just to make your person happy.

Oh, and when you see that your person is working too hard? You sneak into the bathroom cupboard, chew up some toilet paper, and scatter it all over the house to show them that you are ready to party down!

And most important, when your person is sad, you
cuddle up to them and put your nose right on their knee.

That is how you rescue a person.

When I got to Joe's house, I met another dog, who was excited to show me around the place.

His name is Champ. Together, we did our best to make Joe the happiest guy around.

After I had been at Joe's house for a few months, it was time to make it official.

That meant going back to the shelter to sign some papers saying that Joe and I were adopting each other. We even saw a few old friends!

Then I went home with Joe for good.

Not too long after I rescued Joe Biden, he was elected president of the United States. Coincidence? Well, I don't think so!

Because when you rescue someone,
you help them become their very best self.
Now Champ and I live with Joe and Jill at the White House.

There are so many new people that sometimes I get *too* excited.
I even had a friend help me learn to behave myself a little better.

We have a great time together.
We help in the garden.

We defend the house from our most ferocious enemy.

When we are feeling especially dignified, we have afternoon tea.

And because Joe has a tough job, sometimes we check in on him to see if he needs our help.

If you and your family feel like you might need a dog or a cat to rescue you, I think an animal shelter might be worth checking out. Because I know that Joe Biden will care for our country. And in the meantime, Champ and I will care for Joe.

PAST PRESIDENTIAL PETS

While Major is definitely the First Dog, and definitely lives at the White House—Major and his beloved buddy Champ, who has sadly passed away, are *not* the first dogs to live at the White House. In recent years, we've had Bo and Sunny Obama, and George W. Bush's dogs: Spot, Barney, and Miss Beazley. Major isn't even the first presidential *rescue* dog—Lyndon Johnson's pup, Yuki, was given to him by his daughter Luci, who found Yuki at a gas station on Thanksgiving Day.

There have been so many good dogs. James Garfield had a dog named Veto (even though Garfield never vetoed a single bill). Teddy Roosevelt's dog, Pete, once bit the pants off the ambassador to France! John and Abigail Adams had a pup named Satan, and I don't have anything more to say about that.

But if you're like me, you also want to know about all the *other* kinds of animals our presidents had. Well, let's start with the fact that no fewer than TWO of our presidents are rumored to have had pet alligators. Alligators! Legend has it that both Herbert Hoover and John Quincy Adams kept the reptiles at the White House. Adams, who supposedly received his alligator as a gift from the French, kept the pet in a bathtub near the East Room before eventually sending it back to France.

Speaking of gifts: Martin Van Buren was given two baby tigers, but Congress insisted that he send them to a zoo. Thomas Jefferson was similarly gifted two bear cubs that he kept in a cage near the White House's north entrance and would walk on a leash. Theodore Roosevelt had almost a whole zoo himself: In addition to Pete, the pants-loving dog, the Roosevelt family had pigs, cats, a hyena, a lion, a zebra, rats, a badger, a pony, a raccoon, some bears, guinea pigs, a one-legged rooster, and a snake his daughter named Emily Spinach.

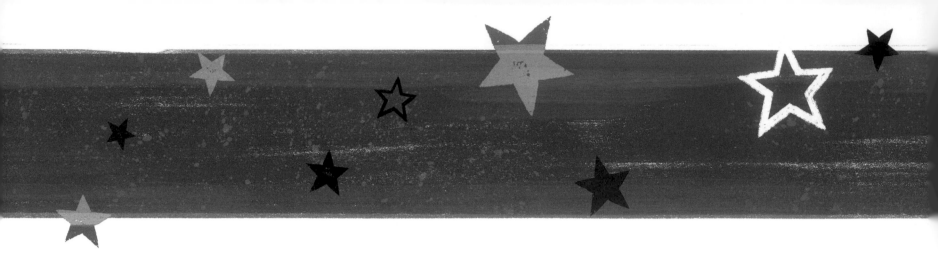

And my favorite pet: Andrew Jackson had a parrot who apparently learned a lot from its extremely cantankerous master because, after the former president died, the bird swore so much at his funeral that it had to be removed from the service.

But let's end with Franklin Delano Roosevelt. I feel like I should mention that FDR had several dogs, including—most importantly for this book—a *very good* German shepherd named Major.

RESOURCES FOR ADOPTING A SHELTER ANIMAL

THE HUMANE SOCIETY OF THE UNITED STATES
www.humanesociety.org/resources/
adopting-animal-shelter-or-rescue-group

ASPCA
www.aspca.org/adopt-pet

OPERATION PAWS FOR HOMES
www.ophrescue.org

ADOPT-A-PET.COM
www.adoptapet.com

THE SHELTER PET PROJECT
www.theshelterpetproject.org/pet-search

BEST FRIENDS ANIMAL SOCIETY
www.bestfriends.org

PETFINDER
www.petfinder.com